# ORCHARD

# ORCHARD

**A year in a Herefordshire cider orchard**

Photographs by Gareth Rees-Roberts

**Logaston Press**

LOGASTON PRESS
Little Logaston Woonton Almeley
Herefordshire HR3 6QH
www.logastonpress.co.uk

First published by Logaston Press 2009
Copyright © Gareth Rees-Roberts 2009
www.garethreesroberts.com

ISBN (paperback) 978 1 906663 26 1
ISBN (hardback) 978 1 906663 27 8

This is number **239** of the limited hardback edition of 500 copies

Typeset by Logaston Press
and printed in Malta by
Gutenberg Press

# A year in a Herefordshire cider orchard

During the mid 1980s many mature cider orchards were being felled and grubbed up in Herefordshire. I used to travel past the 'Big Orchard' at Knapton on a regular basis and one March morning I noticed woodsmoke rising above the trees and feared that a major clearance had begun. The next day I stopped to investigate, and was greatly relieved to discover that the smoke came from a large pile of branches collected together after the annual orchard pruning. The sun's rays were casting through the woodsmoke and I felt compelled to climb over the gate to take a closer look.

I entered the orchard, and found myself in another world. The apple trees seemed to go on forever in all directions and were unusually large for cider stock. Even at this time of year the sheer size and scale of the canopy felt more like a woodland environment than an orchard. The dimensions and formal spacing of the avenues reminded me of the wonderful cloisters at Gloucester Cathedral. I could not resist the opportunity to take some photographs before returning to my car. However, finding my way back was easier said than done, as in my excitement to explore the orchard, I had completely lost my bearings.

My next visit was later in the year on a hot mid-summer's day. Remembering how easy it had been to lose my way, I marked my progress carefully as I wandered further through the trees. The orchard had the appearance of an impressionist's painting, the trees heavy with foliage casting deep shadows along the avenues. The change of atmosphere was extraordinary. This was a fascinating environment to explore, completely insulated from the outside world. There was a deep stillness only occasionally interrupted by the gentle buzzing of insects and the sound of distant birdsong.

The transformation that had taken place in the orchard in the space of just three months had a profound effect upon me. I wanted to continue photographing it on a regular basis, to follow its progress through the course of a year. I eventually located the owner, Glyn Powell, who responded with great enthusiasm for the project.

1987 happened to be a good year for this study, since each season was clearly defined by the weather conditions. January began with clear frosty weather, and I found myself following the strange meandering paths made by the sheep, which seemed to weave random journeys through the avenues of trees. I could not tell how the sheep had formed these well-defined trails, since they never seemed to follow them. The month continued with snow and fog, and the orchard took on a formal grandeur with the seemingly endless lines of trees fading into the mist.

In February the stillness in the orchard was rudely interrupted by the beginning of the annual pruning of the trees. The previous serenity of the orchard vistas soon turned to chaos as the avenues became blocked with felled branches. Early in March the clear-up was well under way and, despite the wet conditions, bonfires were burning in muddy clearings. I became fascinated by the violently uprooted stumps of cankered trees, some of which seemed to be walking down the avenues like surreal triffids. As the weather brightened, aromatic woodsmoke replaced the winter mists, and stillness and order once again returned to the orchard.

There were some spectacular April mornings, when shafts of sunlight fanned out through the trees. Occasionally gentle morning mist would develop into thick fog, leaving me isolated in a damp and increasingly gloomy maze. But by now the orchard was changing colour from muted browns and greys to the lush greens of springtime.

During May the orchard exploded into beautiful blossoms of bridal white tinged with pink. Later the avenues were showered with petals as they gently floated to the ground like confetti. A beekeeper had placed nine hives in the centre of the orchard to maximise the pollination of the trees. One morning I spent over an hour trying to photograph a lesser spotted woodpecker that was flitting from tree to tree, but I could never keep up with it. In contrast to the delicacy of the apple blossom I noticed that all the old uprooted tree stumps had been gathered into an enormous pile in the centre of the orchard, which from a distance took on the appearance of a dinosaur's skeleton.

As spring turned to summer, and the foliage on the apple trees grew thicker, the avenues became increasingly darker, creating a dramatic contrast between deep shadows and brilliant pools of light. The midsummer heat culminated in a violent deluge when, bizarrely, the sun shone through torrential rain. In late summer the screaming of swifts could be heard as they dived after insects above the canopy, and the sheep were removed from the orchard in order to avoid them damaging the apples, now hanging low on heavily laden branches.

From late September the autumn mists began to add a sense of mystery, made all the more fascinating by the appearance of millions of cobwebs. One morning as an early frost was melting, I realised that the whole orchard was carpeted with spiders' webs, and through a gathering mist the heavily laden boughs were eerily festooned with hanging cobwebs. Stepping backwards with my tripod in order to gain an advantageous position, I nearly trod on a hare which shot out from under my feet. It disappeared before I could recover the camera from the nettles.

It seemed as if invisible hands arrived in November to harvest the apples, which covered the ground as far as the eye could see. The evocative aroma of the fallen apples filled the air, giving the senses an eager anticipation of the cider to come. There were rowdy flocks of fieldfares making the most of the rich pickings, but I was never able to get within one hundred yards of them without the alarm being sounded, and the birds would rise like a wave and move further down the avenue.

There were only four occasions when I met anyone else during my year in the 'Big Orchard'. Like the harvesting, the pruning of the apple trees seemed to have been done by invisible hands, though the distant hum of a chainsaw could sometimes be heard across the orchard. One April morning I was surprised by a flock of sheep suddenly appearing through the trees as they were being driven by a shepherd and his dog. The sheep were being cleared from the orchard prior to the annual programme of spraying against pests and disease. A week later I came face to face with a tractor spraying the trees before the buds broke. In mid May, I met the owner, Glyn Powell, admiring the blossom, and then I saw no one until the harvesting in November.

December was cold and frosty, and there was an elegiac feeling in the orchard as my project came full circle. The final apples to be collected were lined up under the trees in blue sacks. One or two trees still clung on to their brilliant red apples when all the others had long since surrendered their fruit to the shaking of the harvesting machinery. The remains of the great pile of old stumps were now decorated with frost, as were the remaining apples lying on the ground.

My final visit of the year was on a freezing afternoon, with a low winter sun shining through the frosted branches of the trees, which was very beautiful but rather sad. As the sun set over the orchard, my project was completed.

A view in May looking north-west over the orchard (in blossom and surrounded by yellow rape fields in the middle distance) from Birley Hill. On an old map it is named as 'The Pantiles Orchard', after the cottages that stand in one corner of the field in which it was planted. However, locally it is referred to either as 'The Old Orchard' or 'The Big Orchard'. The orchard covers over 60 acres (24 hectares), and was planted in 1947 by William Evans & Company with five varieties of cider apples: Brown Norman, Bulmers Norman, Chisel Jersey, Kingston Black and Yarlington Mill. The trees were grafted onto standard rootstock, and rapidly grew to a large size in the rich Herefordshire soil. In 1963 the orchard was purchased by brothers Glyn and Clifford Powell, and the apples were contracted to Bulmers.

**Post Script**

It is now over twenty years since I spent those twelve months photographing the 'Big Orchard', and it has been fascinating editing through more than one thousand negatives and transparencies in preparation for this book. I have felt a certain nostalgia for this project which reinvigorated my passion for photography and encouraged me to meditate more deeply upon the landscape, the seasons, and the passing of time. The orchard still retains a hold on me, and I occasionally return to savour the atmosphere of this special place.

Sadly Glyn Powell, who kindly allowed me the privilege of studying his magnificent orchard, died five years ago, but his widow Molly continues to manage the 'Big Orchard'. The trees were in their fortieth year when I photographed them, and now some of the larger ones have simply collapsed. However, replanting schemes are under way, and the life of the orchard continues.

**The Exhibition**

I was invited to exhibit the orchard series of photographs at the Bleddfa Trust Gallery in October 1987, as part of their celebration of The Year of the Tree. This exhibition was then hired by Bulmers for their Centenary Celebrations, where it was viewed by the Queen, and it was subsequently toured in South Wales by South East Wales Arts. Since then it has been further exhibited in Herefordshire and in Bristol, and there are permanent collections at the Cider Museum, and at the Cider Orchard Restaurant in Hereford.

# Acknowledgements

I would like to thank my wife, Lynden, for her encouragement and advice in the creation of the original exhibition, and in the preparation of the material for the book.

My thanks also go to James Roose-Evans whose invitation to exhibit at the Bleddfa Trust Gallery in October 1987 gave me the impetus to see the project through.

Finally I would like to thank Andy and Karen at Logaston Press for sharing my vision and bringing the work to publication.

Gareth Rees-Roberts

62

66

74